A Robbie Reader

WITHDRAWN

The Fury of Hurricane Andrew, 1992

Karen Bush Gibson

Mitchell Lane
PUBLISHERS

P.O. Box 196
Hockessin, Delaware 19707
Visit us on the web: www.mitchelllane.com
Comments? email us:
mitchelllane@mitchelllane.com

Printing   1   2   3   4   5   6   7   8   9

A Robbie Reader/Natural Disasters
Earthquake in Loma Prieta, California, 1989
The Fury of Hurricane Andrew, 1992
Mt. Vesuvius and the Destruction of Pompeii, A.D. 79
Mudslide in La Conchita, California, 2005
Tsunami Disaster in Indonesia, 2004
Where Did All the Dinosaurs Go?

Library of Congress Cataloging-in-Publication Data
Gibson, Karen Bush.
    The fury of Hurricane Andrew, 1992 / By Karen Gibson.
        p. cm. — (Natural Disasters — what can we learn?)
    "A Robbie Reader."
    Includes bibliographical references and index.
    ISBN 1-58415-416-0 (library bound)
        1. Hurricane Andrew, 1992 — Juvenile literature. 2. Hurricanes — Juvenile literature.
I. Title. II. Series.
QC945.G45 2005
363.34'922'09759 — dc22

                                                                    2005009732

ABOUT THE AUTHOR: Karen Bush Gibson has written extensively for the juvenile market. Her work has appeared in such publications as *Boys' Life* and *Cobblestone*. She is also the author of twenty-four school-library books. Karen lives in Norman, Oklahoma, with her husband and three children.

TABLE OF CONTENTS

Words in **bold** type can be found in the glossary.

Hurricanes can destroy entire homes, leaving the frame of a house or flattening it completely.

MEET HURRICANE ANDREW

How many people can fit in a bedroom closet? For the Walton family of Homestead, Florida, it was a lucky 13. They found out the hard way.

In the early morning of August 24, 1992, the Waltons sat in their living room. While the younger children slept, other family members listened to television and radio news reports. The reports said that the first hurricane (HER-uh-kane) of the season, Hurricane Andrew, was headed for the Miami area. The small town of Homestead was only 20 minutes south of Miami.

The Waltons thought they were ready for Hurricane Andrew. They had been to the supermarket. They bought food that didn't need cooking. They also bought water and other supplies. Other families had done the same.

The Waltons heard the wind and rain outside their house. Suddenly, the noise was louder. Windows in the living room broke into many pieces. The family looked for another room in the house to keep them safe. Glass from windows flew everywhere. A board hit eighth-grader Kenyahna, leaving a huge bruise on her left leg.

Hurricane Andrew packed winds between 145 and 175 miles per hour.

With no other place to go, the family rushed into a windowless bedroom closet. Twenty-year-old Tiffany saw the roof pulling away from the house as they shut the closet door. A loud noise like a train whistle hurt their ears. The Waltons waited out the storm in complete darkness. After a while, they didn't hear anything. Light was peeking under the closet door. Cautiously, they looked out.

They cried when they saw what had happened to their one-story brick home. The roof was gone. The windows were broken. Much of their furniture had been smashed. When the Waltons went outside, they saw that their neighborhood had been destroyed. Tiffany later said, "It was like someone had bombed the neighborhood."

Like many south Florida families, the Waltons were no strangers to hurricanes. They just never thought they would become directly involved. Mother Carol Walton told reporters, "We feel very fortunate to be alive."

A satellite picture shows Hurricane Andrew moving west from Florida, across the Gulf of Mexico.

THE FIRST STORM
OF THE SEASON

Hurricanes are tropical storms with winds above 74 miles per hour (mph). They are the most powerful storms on earth. The eastern and southern coasts of the United States see the most hurricanes, along with the Caribbean (kuh-RIH-bee-yen) islands, which are southeast of the United States. These areas see an average of six hurricanes every year.

Hurricane season starts in June and lasts until the end of November. The 1992 season had been the slowest for Florida in eight years. That began to change on August 14, when a tropical (TRAH-pih-kul) wave formed off the coast of West Africa. A tropical wave is a weather system with wind speeds above 20 mph. This wave increased in strength as it moved westward across the Atlantic Ocean. Three days later, a circular shape formed and

CATEGORY	WIND SPEEDS	DAMAGE
1	74–95 mph	Minimal
2	96–110 mph	Moderate
3	111–130 mph	Extensive
4	131–155 mph	Extreme
5	over 155 mph	Catastrophic

The Saffir-Simpson Hurricane Damage-Potential Scale rates hurricanes on a scale from 1 to 5. Category 1 hurricanes are the weakest, and 5s are the strongest. Hurricanes are considered especially dangerous when they reach category 3.

the winds grew stronger. Tropical Storm Andrew was born. Since 1953, the National Hurricane Center has named all tropical storms and hurricanes. The first one of the year begins with the letter A, the second one with the letter B, and so on.

Tropical Storm Andrew traveled northwest toward the Caribbean Sea. When it reached the warm Gulf Stream near the Bahamas (buh-HAH-muhz), an eye formed in the storm and the wind speed increased even more. Andrew was now a hurricane.

Meteorologists (mee-tee-or-AH-loh-jists) are people who study the weather. They rated Hurricane Andrew between a **category** (KA-tuh-gor-ee) 4 and a category 5. A category 5 is the worst kind of hurricane. Andrew was at its strongest as it passed over the northern Bahamas. Sixteen-foot ocean waves caused severe damage and killed four people.

Studying hurricanes is a hard job. Meteorologists try to guess where a hurricane is going and how much harm it will do.

They study pictures from **satellites** (SA-tuh-lites). They also use instruments that measure wind, rain, and air pressure. The National Hurricane Center and the National Oceanic

A technician checks a door on a weather satellite. Behind the door is an instrument that will test temperature and moisture in Earth's atmosphere.

Special airplanes fly into hurricanes to gather information.

(oh-shee-AA-nik) and Atmospheric (at-muhss-FEAR-ik) Administration (NOAA) are two groups that study storms. Sometimes NOAA or the Air Force Reserve flies special airplanes into hurricanes to collect information. All this information helps people decide what to do. In the case of Hurricane Andrew, meteorologists told people they should try to leave south Florida before the hurricane arrived.

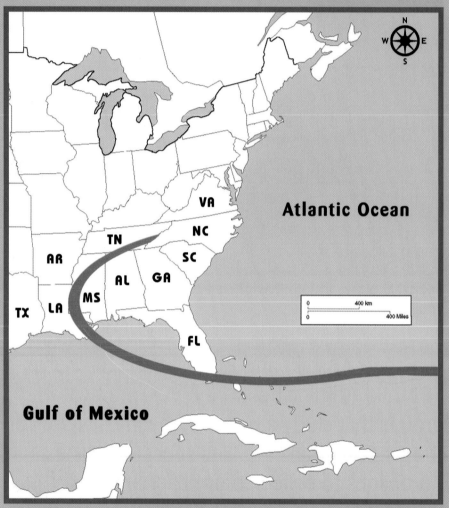

The red line shows the path of Hurricane Andrew. It struck Florida (FL) first and continued its path through the Gulf of Mexico, hitting land again in Louisiana (LA). It went through Mississippi (MS) to the northern tip of Alabama (AL) before it died down in the southeastern part of Tennessee (TN). By the time it reached North Carolina (NC) and Virginia (VA), it was just a heavy rainstorm.

HURRICANE ANDREW COMES TO FLORIDA

Hurricane Andrew reached Florida with winds of 145 mph. Wind **gusts** may have been as high as 175 mph. Weather instruments called **anemometers** (a-nuh-MAH-meh-ters) measured the speed of the wind. When the wind speed reached 164 mph at the National Hurricane Center, the anemometer broke.

The high winds blew out electricity everywhere and left people in darkness. The storm was so strong that it knocked a two-**ton** radar **antenna** (an-TEN-uh) from the roof of the National Hurricane Center. At Biscayne (bis-KANE) Bay, located just south of Miami, water levels reached 17 feet above sea level. The hurricane picked up a 350-ton sunken ship from the ocean floor. Andrew threw the ship on top of a natural **reef** 700 feet away.

Many people listened to the warnings from the National Hurricane Center. They taped or boarded the windows to their homes to protect them from breaking. Then they packed. Many things had to be left behind. The roads were crowded with people driving north to escape the storm. Other families went to nearby hurricane shelters such as school gymnasiums.

The Mullins family waited out the storm in their fish store. The store's concrete walls began shaking and water poured in through holes in the roof. LaVerne Mullins told reporters what happened next. "We moved into the fish locker," she said. "Now we all smell like fish, but we are all alive."

Hurricane Andrew moved across Florida at the rate of 18 mph. It destroyed nearly everything in a path 25 miles wide.

Southern Florida looked like a war zone. Pieces of metal and wood from smashed buildings lay on the ground. The towns of Homestead and Florida City lost 3,000 acres of farmland. Andrew ripped lemon, lime, and avocado trees from the ground.

Fifteen people died from Hurricane Andrew. At least 25 others lost their lives to causes related to the hurricane. Nearly all of the mobile homes in the area were destroyed. More than 250,000 people lost their homes. The next day, Florida governor Lawton Chiles visited the storm areas. He had never seen anything like it. He said it looked like a powerful bomb had exploded.

More than 250,000 people lost their homes in Hurricane Andrew.

Hurricanes damage all kinds of personal property, from boats, homes, and cars to photographs and other mementos that can't be replaced.

PICKING UP THE PIECES

Hurricane Andrew left Florida around 9:00 in the morning on August 24. It was weaker, a category 3 hurricane now. It moved across the Gulf of Mexico toward Louisiana. Many people in Louisiana and on the Texas coast were asked to leave for safety reasons.

Hurricane Andrew reached south-central Louisiana around 5:00 A.M. on the 26th, only 48 hours after it began its trip across Florida. Its winds were now 115 mph, with 140 mph gusts.

Hurricanes often bring a lot of rain. Hurricane Andrew was no exception, though it moved over Florida too quickly to drench the area. It was different in Louisiana, where more than 11 inches of rain fell in places.

CHAPTER FOUR

A man surveys hurricane damage to an apartment building.

Eight-foot storm tides led to widespread flooding. Tornadoes from hurricanes are also a danger. Although no tornadoes were reported in Florida, several of them struck Louisiana, causing two deaths and much damage.

Back in Florida, people left the storm shelters to check on their homes. Many people lost everything. South Florida was declared a disaster area. The U.S. government sent people and supplies to help. After medical care, the most important needs were for safe water, food, and shelter.

Meanwhile, Hurricane Andrew was losing power. On August 27, it was downgraded to a tropical storm. It curved northeast the following day, where it joined several other weather systems. They dumped heavy rain on the Mid-Atlantic states.

The U.S. government sent soldiers and supplies to help victims of Hurricane Andrew.

LESSONS FROM HURRICANE ANDREW

In 1992, Hurricane Andrew was the costliest natural disaster the United States had ever seen. Its long-term costs have been estimated at as much as $40 billion.

Both Florida and Louisiana suffered severe damage. Overturned boats leaked fuel and oil into the ocean. Almost two million fish from the waters of Louisiana died. Hurricane Andrew hit **fragile** (FRA-jil) wetlands in both states. Another fragile area was the coral reefs off the coast of Florida. One-third of the reefs at Biscayne National Park were damaged. Some were 200 years old.

Businesses were also affected. Louisiana's $400 million sugarcane industry suffered. One

Relief organizations such as the Salvation Army brought food and water and provided shelter to the victims of Hurricane Andrew.

of the biggest employers in Homestead, the U.S. Air Force base, was also severely damaged. About 100,000 people moved away from south Florida.

Some people, including the Lampert family, decided to stay. Hurricane Andrew had sent a neighbor's shed through 19-year-old Annette Lampert's bedroom. The family lost their roof and a wall of their house. Later, they

Many volunteers helped distribute items to those
in need.

moved into a new house with new furniture.
While they were happy to have a new home,
they still missed things that couldn't be
replaced, such as photos and other personal
mementos (muh-MEN-toes).

In early 1995 (nearly three years after
Hurricane Andrew), the last 180 people who
had lost their homes moved out of a temporary
trailer park into permanent dwellings. One of
them was security guard Mack Johnson. He was

People at the National Hurricane Center are able to track hurricanes before they hit.

happy to say good-bye to Trailer #299 in Coral Rock Trailer Park and move into an apartment.

People who study hurricanes say that the damage could have been even worse. Hurricane Andrew was a relatively small storm compared to others.

Since record keeping began in 1851, the busiest hurricane season was 1933. That year, 21 storms were named. The year 2005 was shaping up to pass that record.

In late August 2005, Hurricane Katrina drowned parts of Louisiana, Mississippi, and Alabama. Thousands of people were killed, and hundreds of thousands were made homeless. Whole towns, including the city of New Orleans, were destroyed. Less than one month later, Hurricane Rita pounded southeastern Texas and parts of Louisiana again. It would take billions of dollars to rebuild. As happened in Florida after Hurricane Andrew, thousands of people would never return to their hometowns.

Hurricanes can ruin homes and belongings, but they can't take away the human spirit.

CHRONOLOGY

August 14, 1992 A tropical wave forms off the coast of West Africa.

August 17 The tropical wave grows into Tropical Storm Andrew.

August 22 Tropical Storm Andrew turns into a hurricane.

August 23 Hurricane Andrew hits the Bahamas, killing four people.

August 24 Hurricane Andrew hits Florida, killing 15 people and leading to the deaths of at least 25 more.

August 26 Hurricane Andrew reaches Louisiana, leading to flooding and tornadoes.

August 27 Hurricane Andrew is downgraded to a tropical storm and heads northeast.

August 28 Andrew joins a group of other storms, bringing rain to the Mid-Atlantic states.

OTHER MAJOR U.S. HURRICANES

1900 Galveston, Texas, 8,000–10,000 dead (deadliest in U.S. history)

1926 "Great Miami Hurricane," 373 dead

1928 "San Felipe Hurricane," Florida and the Caribbean, 3,411 dead

1935 "Labor Day Hurricane," Florida Keys, 408 dead

1938 New England hurricane, 600 dead

1957 Hurricane Audrey, Texas/Louisiana, 394 dead

1969 Hurricane Camille, southeast United States, 256 dead

1972 Hurricane Agnes, Florida/Georgia, 134 dead

1989 Hurricane Hugo, South and North Carolina, 71 dead

1999 Hurricane Floyd, North Carolina, 57 dead

2004 Hurricanes Charley, Frances, Ivan, and Jeanne pound Florida within a two-month period, killing 70 in the U.S.

2005 Hurricanes Katrina and Rita strike Louisiana, Mississippi, Florida, and Texas, killing over a thousand and leaving hundreds of thousands homeless

FIND OUT MORE

Books

Berger, Melvin. *Hurricanes Have Eyes But Can't See: And Other Amazing Facts About Wild Weather.* New York: Scholastic, 2004.

Cole, Johanna. *The Magic School Bus Inside a Hurricane.* New York: Scholastic, 1996.

Morris, Neil. *Hurricanes and Tornadoes.* New York: Crabtree, 1998.

Sherrow, Victoria. *Hurricane Andrew: Nature's Rage.* Berkeley Heights, New Jersey: Enslow Publishers, 1998.

Simon, Seymour. *Hurricanes.* New York: HarperCollins Publishers, 2003.

Wiesner, David. *Hurricane.* New York: Clarion Books, 1992.

On the Internet

Miami Museum of Science
http://www.miamisci.org/hurricane/
National Hurricane Center for Kids
http://www.nhc.noaa.gov/HAW2/english/kids.shtml
NOAA Education
http://www.education.noaa.gov/sweather.html

GLOSSARY

anemometer (a-nuh-MAH-meh-ter)—a scientific tool used to measure the wind's speed.

antenna (an-TEN-uh)—a device that receives signals from radio, television, or satellites.

category (KA-tuh-gor-ee)—a group or section into which things are organized.

fragile (FRA-jil)—delicate or easily broken.

gusts (GUHSTS)—sudden, strong blasts of wind.

mementos (muh-MEN-toes)—items kept to remember a place, an experience, or a person.

meteorologist (mee-tee-or-AH-loh-jist)—someone who studies the weather.

reef (REEF)—a strip of rock, sand, or coral close to the surface of the ocean.

satellites (SA-tuh-lites)—objects that orbit the earth and send signals.

ton (TUHN)—a measure of weight that equals 2,000 pounds.

INDEX